HOMONYMS

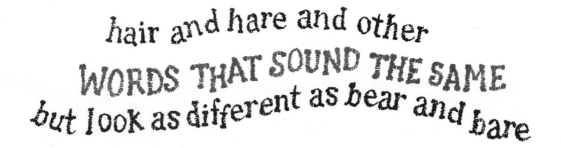

hair and hare and other
WORDS THAT SOUND THE SAME
but look as different as bear and bare

HOMONYMS

Joan
Hanson

Published by
Lerner Publications Company
Minneapolis, Minnesota

For Farmor and Farfar

International Standard Book Number: 0-8225-0277-1
Library of Congress Catalog Card Number: 72-1121

Second Printing 1973

hom·o·nym (HAHM-uh-nim) A word that sounds the same as another word but has a different spelling and meaning. These words are homonyms: *see* and *sea; made* and *maid; dear* and *deer.*

Flee

Flea

Herd

Heard

Hare

Hair

Son

Sun

Scent

Cent

Flower

Flour

Peak

Peek

Pain

Pane

Rain

Rein

Bear

Bare

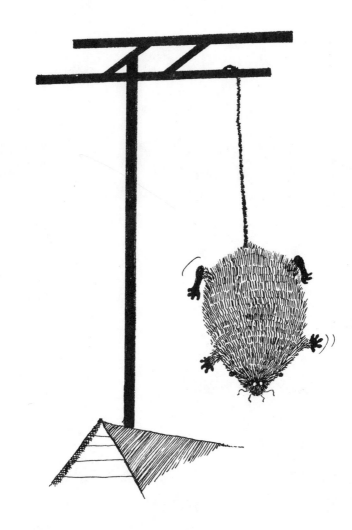

Tail

Tale

Rap

Wrap

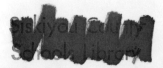

Wring

Ring

BOOKS IN THIS SERIES

ANTONYMS
hot and cold and other
WORDS THAT ARE DIFFERENT
as night and day

MORE ANTONYMS
wild and tame and other
WORDS THAT ARE AS DIFFERENT IN MEANING
as work and play

HOMONYMS
hair and hare and other
WORDS THAT SOUND THE SAME
but look as different as bear and bare

MORE HOMONYMS
steak and stake and other
WORDS THAT SOUND THE SAME
but look as different as chili and chilly

HOMOGRAPHS
bow and bow and other
WORDS THAT LOOK THE SAME
but sound as different as sow and sow

HOMOGRAPHIC HOMOPHONES
fly and fly and other
WORDS THAT LOOK AND SOUND THE SAME
but are as different in meaning as bat and bat

British-American SYNONYMS
french fries and chips and other
WORDS THAT MEAN THE SAME THING
but look and sound
as different as truck and lorry

MORE SYNONYMS
shout and yell and other
WORDS THAT MEAN THE SAME THING
but look and sound
as different as loud and noisy

*We specialize in producing quality books for
young people. For a complete list please write*

LERNER PUBLICATIONS COMPANY
241 First Avenue North, Minneapolis, Minnesota 55401